W9-CFO-832

Natural Treatment of Fibroid Tumors and Endometriosis

Effective natural solutions for relieving the heavy bleeding, cramps and infertility that accompany these common female problems

Susan M. Lark, M.D.

Keats Publishing, Inc. New Canaan, Connecticut

ABOUT THE AUTHOR

Susan M. Lark, M.D. is a noted authority on women's health care and preventive medicine. Dr. Lark, a graduate of Northwestern University Medical School, is on the clinical faculty of Stanford University Medical School. She is the author of many bestselling books on the natural approach to women's health, including *Fibroid Tumors and Endometriosis*, from which this Good Health Guide is excerpted.

NOTE: The information in this booklet is meant to complement, not replace the advice of your physician. It is very important for women with fibroid tumors or endometriosis to have these problems evaluated and monitored by a physician.

ISBN: 0-87983-690-3

Printed in the United States of America

Good Health Guides are published by
Keats Publishing, Inc.
27 Pine Street (Box 876)
New Canaan, Connecticut 06840-0876

Contents

INTRODUCTION

Fibroids and endometriosis are diseases that affect many women during their prime reproductive years, most often from their twenties through their forties. These are the years when women are starting and developing their careers and families—a time of new and exciting life experiences. Energy and a zest for life are often at their peak. These women work at energy levels they may never achieve again; though many will remain active into their older years, they will tend to live more sensibly and at a more moderate pace.

Yet, for the millions of younger women who suffer from symptoms caused by fibroids or endometriosis, the quality of life often declines significantly. These women have recurrent painful and unpleasant symptoms that jeopardize their ability to work, care for children, enjoy personal relationships, and even engage in sexual intercourse during a period of several days to several weeks each month. Fibroids and endometriosis are common causes of infertility and affect the ability of some women to bear children.

Although the actual disease processes are quite different—fibroids are benign tumors in the uterus, while endometriosis is a condition that causes inflammation and scarring in the pelvis—they are often triggered by the same mechanisms. Hormonal imbalances, stress, and nutritional factors play major roles in both problems. Why some women develop one disease rather than the other or why other women develop both diseases at the same time is not known. Symptoms of the two diseases are fairly similar. As a result, they are often treated by the same types of drugs and surgical procedures, although the overlap is certainly not total.

Women with severe fibroids or endometriosis have histori-cally been treated with many different drug and hormonal therapies in an attempt to control the symptoms. These women faced a high risk of eventually having a hysterec-tomy. Luckily, women today can often avoid this grim scenario. A healthy lifestyle can play a beneficial role in relieving and preventing the symptoms of fibroids and endometriosis. New medical therapies that have become available during the past 15 years are more effective than those used in the past. I discuss both the self-care and medical therapies for fibroids and endometriosis in this book.

Over the past 20 years, I have worked with many patients who suffered from fibroids and endometriosis. Many of my patients have benefited from a self-care approach to their problems. While medication and even surgery may be neces-sary to treat women with more advanced disease, the impor-tance of practicing beneficial lifestyle habits cannot be underestimated for symptom relief and prevention. I have spent years researching the use of diet, nutrition, and many other techniques as part of a complete approach to treating these problems. I have learned specific acupressure points, yoga stretches, exercise routines, and various approaches to stress management in order to give my patients many differ-ent self-care options. My goal with patients has always been to provide the information, education, and resources to help them relieve their symptoms through becoming healthier women and then maintaining this state through healthy life-style practices.

This fibroid and endometriosis self-help program is practical and easy to follow. You can use it by itself or in conjunction with a medical program. While working with a physician is necessary to establish a definitive diagnosis of these two prob-lems, and medical therapy may still be necessary for women with moderate to severe symptoms, the importance of a good self-help program cannot be underestimated. For many women, this book can help speed up the diagnostic process. My self-help techniques can play a major role in reducing the severity of your symptoms and preventing recurrences of the disease process. The feeling of wellness that can be yours with a self-help program will radiate out and touch your whole life. You will have more time and energy to enjoy your work, family, and other pleasures in life. Most of my patients tell me that their lives have been positively transformed by these beneficial self-help techniques.

WHAT ARE FIBROIDS?

Fibroids are one of the most common female health problems affecting women during their reproductive years. They occur primarily in women in their twenties through their late forties. Their incidence can occasionally extend through menopause, affecting women in their fifties and beyond. Fibroid tumors of the uterus are found in at least 40 percent of American women who reach menopause. Over time, tens of millions of women develop these growths.

Not all fibroids require medical intervention. In fact, many women with fibroids go through years of annual pelvic exams in which the physician simply notes the fibroids on the chart, for they are causing no problems whatsoever. However, approximately 50 percent of women with fibroids develop symptoms severe enough to have a major impact on quality of life. In my practice, fibroids are a very common finding that often coexists with other gynecological complaints such as PMS, menstrual cramps, ovarian cysts, endometriosis, and heavy menstrual flow.

Fibroids are benign growths that can actually arise in muscle tissue anywhere in the body but are found most commonly in the uterus. Unlike cancer, they do not invade surrounding tissue or distant organs, nor will untreated fibroids kill the affected person. In fact, less than one-half of 1 percent of fibroids ever become cancerous; this usually occurs in postmenopausal women. Instead, these benign muscular tumors tend to remain within the confines of the uterine tissue. However, as they grow larger, they can extend their range and put pressure on neighboring organs and tissues. As the tumor grows, the surrounding tissue is condensed and compressed, forming a type of capsule around the tumor.

Fibroids can vary in number and size. Often multiple fibroids arise over time. Physicians performing surgery on fibroids have found as many as several hundred tumors on a single woman. Fibroids range in size from tiny pinpoint areas of tissue to rare cases of tumors weighing up to 25 pounds or more.

Significant growth of the fibroids usually causes the entire uterus to enlarge. Often a gynecologist feels a firm, irregularly enlarged uterus with smoothly rounded protrusions arising from the uterine wall. Gynecologists tend to describe fibroids in terms of the uterine enlargement caused by pregnancy. A woman with fibroids may be described by her physician as having a "12- to 14-week-size uterus" or even a "20- to 24-week-size uterus," which approximates a 6-month pregnancy in a woman with very large tumors. Interestingly, not all large fibroids cause symptoms. If the fibroids grow in a way that does not cause pressure on neighboring organs, a woman can live with large fibroids for many years without needing medical care.

Most fibroids (95 percent) occur in the body of the uterus; the remaining 5 percent arise from the cervix. Fibroids can arise in different locations within the uterus. *Submucosal* fibroids grow on the inside of the uterus and extend into the uterine cavity from the lining of the uterus, or endometrium. *Intramural* fibroids grow within the uterine wall; *subserosal* fibroids grow on the outside of the uterus, in the lining between the uterus and the pelvic cavity. Some fibroids can grow large enough to extend their boundaries from the uterus into the pelvic ligaments. Each may even develop a long, narrow stalk as it extends into the pelvic cavity. Occasionally fibroids grow large enough to press on the bowel or bladder, or through the cervix, where they can be mistaken for cervical polyps during a gynecological examination. Rarely, they attach to the intestinal wall and become parasitic on the tissue of the bowel lining. Thus, fibroids can grow in a variety of locations from the uterine muscle and can impinge on different pelvic organs depending on their pattern of growth.

RISK FACTORS THAT INCREASE THE LIKELIHOOD OF FIBROIDS

Fibroids are much more sensitive to estrogen stimulation than is normal muscle tissue. If the tendency toward fibroid tumors exists, stimulation by estrogen can cause these tumors to grow. They can grow rapidly and become very large when estrogen levels are high, such as during pregnancy, or when exposed to birth control pills containing high doses of estrogen. Normally, fibroids shrink and even disappear during menopause when the estrogen levels produced by the body decline greatly. However, the use of estrogen replacement therapy can reactivate and stimulate the growth of fibroids in some postmenopausal women, occasionally leading to severe complications such as heavy menstrual bleeding. Even excessive body weight can increase fibroid growth, because women who are overweight tend to secrete high levels of estrogen.

Fibroids also coexist in women who show other signs of elevated estrogen, such as anovulatory cycles—menstrual cycles in which only estrogen is secreted without progesterone. These cycles are often seen in women under severe emotional and physical stress, during the transition into menopause, or with endometrial hyperplasia (an overgrowth of the uterine lining that occurs when estrogen levels are high). These conditions are associated with an increased risk of uterine cancer. Women with uterine fibroids are also at an increased risk of developing uterine cancer.

Even poor nutritional habits can elevate estrogen levels by inhibiting the body's ability to break down and excrete excess estrogen. The liver has a dual role in digestion— processing the foods that we take in through our daily meals and regulating hormonal levels by deactivating hormones. A high-stress diet—one that is too rich in saturated fats from meats and dairy products, alcohol, sugar, or other difficult-to-handle foods—may overwork the liver, leaving it unable to break down the hormones efficiently. This leads to the elevated levels of estrogen that can trigger fibroids.

Though estrogen is secreted by the ovaries in a form called estradiol, the liver metabolizes estrogen so it can be eliminated from the body effectively, first by converting estradiol to an intermediary form called estrone, and finally to estriol. The liver's ability to efficiently convert estradiol to estriol is important because estriol is the safest and least chemically active form of estrogen. In contrast, estrone and estradiol are very active stimulants of breast and uterine tissue and may worsen estrogen-dependent problems like PMS, fibrocystic breast disease, fibroids, endometriosis, and even breast cancer. Besides metabolizing estrogen to safer forms, the liver helps to keep the levels of estrogen circulating in the blood from getting too high. Thus, healthy liver function is necessary for estrogen metabolism.

The liver is also dependent on an adequate supply of vitamin B to carry out its tasks. If B vitamins are lacking in the diet, the liver does not have the raw materials it needs to perform its metabolic tasks and regulate estrogen levels.

An inherited tendency toward the development of fibroids seems to exist. Women of African or Asian descent have a two to fivefold greater risk of developing fibroids than do Caucasian women. The tendency to develop fibroid tumors often runs in families. Many patients tell me that their mothers or sisters have fibroids, too; this is a relatively common story when a physician takes a medical history. Fibroids also seem to be more prevalent in women who haven't had children. Conversely, the more children you have, the less likely you are to develop fibroids.

In summary, though risk factors such as racial and family background cannot be changed, fibroids can be greatly influenced by the hormones we use, the foods we eat, and personal stress. Healthy lifestyle habits can reduce your exposure to such factors.

Symptoms of Fibroids

Though many women never have symptoms from fibroids, 50 percent of the women with fibroids require medical help. Depending on size and location, fibroids can cause a variety of symptoms; the most common include bleeding, pain, and infertility. Check with your physician if you have these symptoms and suspect that fibroids could be the cause.

Bleeding. Approximately one-third of women with fibroids suffer from abnormal uterine bleeding. Many women develop heavier menstrual flow that often lasts more days than normal. Some women develop irregular bleeding between periods. In my practice, I have seen women with fibroids develop such heavy bleeding that they actually become anemic. If not treated rapidly, heavy bleeding can cause significant health problems such as weakness, tiredness, and shortness of breath on exertion. If the bleeding continues unchecked, a woman can end up requiring hospitalization and a surgical procedure to stop the problem. Check with your physician if you notice changes in your bleeding pattern. Any significant changes in menstrual flow must be evaluated, since the cause could be rapidly growing fibroids or another serious medical problem.

There are several reasons why fibroids cause this heavy bleeding pattern. The growth of fibroids may expand the area of the cavity by 10 to 15 times, thus providing a greater surface area to bleed each month. They can also push against the blood vessels in the uterus and disrupt the normal blood flow; this pattern occurs with intramural fibroids. It may be that the presence of an intramural fibroid restricts uterine contractions and interferes with the constriction of the endometrial blood vessels, allowing excessive bleeding.

The high levels of estrogen that stimulate the growth of fibroids can also disrupt normal functioning of the uterine lining. Usually the normal balance between estrogen and progesterone regulates the amount of menstrual blood loss. When estrogen levels are elevated, blood loss from the endometrium increases, adding to the excessive flow already caused by the fibroids.

Pain. Many women with fibroids experience symptoms of pressure and pain, sometimes feeling a sense of progressive pelvic fullness or a dragging sensation. This is most commonly due to slowly enlarging intramural or subserosal fibroids. Such fibroids may be easy to feel during a pelvic or abdominal exam. In fact, my patients with very large fibroids are often astonished at the ease with which they can feel their own fibroids through the abdominal wall.

Fibroids that grow to the point of creating pressure on other pelvic structures may affect both bladder and bowel function. When pressing against the bladder, a fibroid tumor can cause a reduction in bladder capacity, resulting in frequent urination and urgency. Occasionally, pressure on a ureter (the tube that brings urine from the kidney to the bladder) may lead to kidney damage. Fibroids that press on the bowels may cause constipation or hemorrhoids.

For some women, the pain of fibroids takes a more serious and disabling form. First, fibroids can cause unpleasant cramps. In addition, when a fibroid enlarges rapidly, acute, severe pain can result if there is degeneration or inflammation within the body of the fibroid itself. This is not an uncommon occurrence during pregnancy. Occasionally, a fibroid may twist on its stalk, a movement that can be extremely painful. A fibroid tumor that begins to prolapse downward through the cervix can cause dull, low-midline pelvic pain as well as pain during intercourse.

Infertility. Fibroids may be the cause in as many as 5 to 10 percent of infertility cases. Fibroids may inhibit implantation of the fertilized egg in the uterine lining by altering transport of the sperm, compressing the fallopian tube, or disrupting the lining of the uterus. In addition, fibroids may possibly cause spontaneous abortion during the first three months of pregnancy, either by distorting the uterine cavity or by altering the blood flow that would normally be needed to nourish the growing fetus. In any case, women with a history of infertility who wish to conceive should be carefully evaluated to determine the size and location of any preexisting fibroids.

Diagosis of Fibroids

Fibroids can be diagnosed in several ways. Most commonly a preliminary diagnosis is made through an abdominal and pelvic examination. A uterus that contains fibroids will often feel enlarged, with an irregular contour. The uterus will probably have a hard, lumpy feel, although some fibroids may feel more soft and cystic. A diagnosis based on an abdominal and pelvic exam is correct about 85 percent of the time. Other conditions, such as an ovarian cancer or cyst, a pelvic inflammatory mass, a mass originating in the bowel, or even an early pregnancy, may occasionally be mistaken for a fibroid.

For further diagnosis, a pelvic ultrasound can be done. This is a visualization technique to identify lesions by their shape and density. Fibroids have specific visual characteristics on ultrasound that differentiate them from cysts and other structures. Tests, such as the intravenous pyelogram and barium enema, are imaging techniques used for the bowel and urinary tract. A blood count, urinalysis, and checks for blood in bowel movements may also be done when a physician undertakes a thorough evaluation of the pelvic mass.

When bleeding is the main symptom of a possible fibroid, the physician may take a tissue sample of the uterine lining or endometrium for diagnostic purposes. This is usually done in the physician's office through either an endometrial biopsy (which uses a small sampling device) or a D&C (which uses larger tools). The D&C also allows the physician to actually feel the irregularity of the endometrial surface typical of fibroid tumors. Once a definitive diagnosis of the fibroid is made, effective treatment can be instituted to alleviate the symptoms, promote regression of the tumor, and prevent more from forming.

WHAT IS ENDOMETRIOSIS?

Endometriosis refers to the condition in which cells comprising the lining of the uterus, called the endometrium, break away and grow outside the uterine cavity, implanting themselves in the pelvis. These implants can occur in many locations within the pelvis, including the ovaries, ligaments of the uterus, cervix, appendix, bowel, and bladder. Occasionally, these cells can even invade distant structures such as a lung or armpit. Like the regular lining of the uterus, these implants respond to hormonal stimulation and can cause bleeding in the pelvic cavity. Unlike normal menstrual bleeding, implant bleeding cannot leave the body through the vaginal opening during menstruation. Instead, blood from the endometrial implants remains trapped in the pelvis where it can cause inflammation, cysts, scar tissue, and other structural damage to the many tissues and organs in this area.

The endometrial implants can assume a variety of shapes and colors. They can include lesions that are tiny pinpoint areas of bleeding; white opaque plaques; or small lesions, rust or dark brown in color, that are described as "mulberry" or "raspberry" in appearance. Some medical textbooks describe these dark areas as looking like "powder burns." Fibrous tissue often grows around these lesions, giving them a puckered appearance. In more advanced cases, adhesions (scar tissue) develop around the implants. The scar tissue can be so dense that it obliterates the normal pelvic structures. Endometrial implants on the ovary can form cysts; these cysts are often called "chocolate cysts" because they are filled with a thick, dark brown fluid that is actually old blood. The inflammatory changes, scarring, and tissue damage associated with endometrial implants can destroy and distort the normal pelvic tissues in a way that causes significant problems for affected women.

Endometriosis is considered an important gynecological problem because it can cause chronic pain and discomfort in younger women during their prime reproductive years. In fact, it is found primarily in menstruating women from age 20 to 45, with its peak incidence in the thirties and forties. It is not, however, limited to this age group; endometriosis can be found in teenagers and even occasionally in postmenopausal women, since the estrogen used in hormone replacement therapy can reactivate the endometrial implants. Endometriosis is a relatively common problem, affecting as many as five million American women (or 7 to 15 percent of the female population). It is a major cause of chronic pain and severe menstrual cramps in younger women, affecting over 50 percent of those in their teens. The pelvic damage caused by endometriosis can also hamper childbearing. In fact, 20 to 66 percent of women with endometriosis experience infertility, a finding based on medical research and clinical studies.

RISK FACTORS THAT INCREASE THE LIKELIHOOD OF ENDOMETRIOSIS

Whatever the cause of endometriosis, a number of factors can predispose a woman toward developing this problem. Though endometriosis can occur in women of any type or background during their active reproductive years, it does seem to occur more frequently in high-achieving career women who suffer from significant personal and career stress. Significant stress can disrupt the delicate hormonal balance in women, as well as weaken immune function, which can allow endometrial implants to grow and spread. Childlessness is also a risk factor for endometriosis and, in fact, pregnancy does seem to offer protection against developing the symptoms of this disease. This may be in part because women with multiple pregnancies have fewer menstrual cycles than do childless women, and thus have far less stimulation of the implants by the normal monthly hormonal fluctuations.

Endometriosis occurs primarily in Caucasian women, although many cases are found among women of Asian and African heritage and those of other ethnic and racial backgrounds. A familial predisposition to endometriosis seems to exist, and 8 to 10 percent of patients with endometriosis have mothers or sisters similarly afflicted. Women who suffer from recurrent stress to the immune system, such as chronic infections, may also be more prone to the development and spread of endometriosis. Weakened immune systems may be unable to control the proliferation of the implants as well as the inflammation and scarring that they cause in the pelvic area.

As mentioned earlier, the endometrial implants are stimulated by estrogen. As with fibroids, the excessive use of any food that elevates estrogen levels is a risk factor for worsening the spread and symptoms of endometriosis. The liver controls the levels of estrogen circulating through the body. It is responsible for deactivating estrogen chemically so that it can be excreted from the body. If the liver is unable to carry out this task efficiently because of a diet high in alcohol, fat, dairy products, red meat, sugar, and chocolate, estrogen levels can become elevated and worsen endometriosis. To deactivate estrogen, the liver also needs sufficient levels of certain B-complex vitamins, so a vitamin B deficiency can exacerbate the problem. Even obesity can contribute to endometriosis because overweight women tend to produce higher levels of estrogen.

The use of estrogen therapy is contraindicated for women with endometriosis. Such women should not be given estrogen-dominant birth control pills, and estrogen replacement therapy should be used very cautiously during the postmenopausal period. Otherwise, women are at risk of restimulating the implants, which often regress after menopause when estrogen levels decline.

In summary, many of the factors that predispose women to the spread of endometriosis can be modified and even eliminated through changes in lifestyle. This is true even for women whose racial, ethnic, and family background would put them in a higher risk category.

SYMPTOMS OF ENDOMETRIOSIS

Endometriosis can present with a wide variety of symptoms. The types of symptoms and degree of severity depend on where the implants are located. Interestingly, 30 percent of women with endometriosis experience no symptoms at all and find out only incidentally that they have this problem. Typically this happens if the implants are located away from nerves and other sensitive structures within the pelvis. The other 70 percent of affected women can find endometriosis quite disabling, experiencing severe and recurrent symptoms. The most common symptoms found in women with endometriosis are:

Menstrual Cramps and Pain. Approximately 60 percent of women with endometriosis suffer from progressively worsening menstrual cramps. Menstrual cramp problems caused by endometriosis often begin when women are in their twenties and thirties, although they can affect teenagers, also. Symptoms may occur for as long as two weeks premenstrually and can continue through menstruation. Cramps caused by endometriosis may be extremely painful and may not respond to the usual menstrual cramp medications, such as birth control pills or anti-inflammatory drugs.

The chronic pelvis pain caused by endometriosis may be due not only to stimulation of and bleeding from the implants, but also to the adhesions and pelvic scarring that inflammation in these implants causes over time. Many women with advanced endometriosis are discovered during surgery to have thick scar tissue that can deform or even obliterate the normal structure of the ovaries, ligaments, bowels, and other pelvic structures.

Some women with endometriosis also suffer from pain at ovulation. Mid-month ovulation usually causes no pain in most women. However, in women with endometriosis, hormonal stimulation of the implants can cause a slight bleeding with subsequent irritation of nerve endings in the pelvic cavity. This can lead to pelvic pain lasting about two days.

Dyspareunia. This means pain on sexual intercourse. It can occur when there is endometrial invasion of the uterosacral ligaments or of a pouch located behind the uterus called the cul-de-sac, or pouch of Douglas. Implants growing in this area can push the uterus in a tilted-back position that doctors call retroversion. When the uterus is pulled backward out of its normal position, deep vaginal penetration during intercourse can become very painful. In fact, the pain can be so severe that sexual intercourse becomes too uncomfortable to participate in. Implants in the cul-de-sac can also be responsible for the low back pain that affects some women during menstruation.

Infertility. Endometriosis is a common cause of infertility. Medical studies have estimated that approximately 30 percent of women with endometriosis are unable to conceive. Endometriosis can cause infertility by scarring and obstructing the fallopian tubes so severely that the tubes cannot pick up the egg, or by scarring the ovaries so extensively that ovulation is prevented. In the general population, approximately 10 percent of women are estimated to be infertile. For women who have never been pregnant and still want to conceive and bear a child, this may be one of the more difficult emotional aspects surrounding endometriosis. Accomplishing a successful pregnancy may require long-term medical care, and even this effort does not always succeed. Medical studies have found, not surprisingly, that the milder the case, the more likely a woman is to become pregnant after treatment of the endometriosis.

Abnormal Bleeding. Abnormal bleeding, including premenstrual spotting as well as excessive menstrual flow, occurs in approximately one-third of all women with endometriosis. In some cases of endometriosis, the menstrual cycles may also be irregular. Bleeding abnormalities in women with endometriosis may be due to lack of ovulation. In anovulatory cycles, progesterone is not secreted. Progesterone has an important effect on the uterine lining during the normal menstrual cycle and helps to limit the amount of blood flow. When progesterone is missing, blood flow can be excessive. When excessive bleeding or spotting happens frequently, iron-deficiency anemia may occur. Women with anemia due to excessive bleeding may find that their energy levels drop and that they lose stamina and endurance, in addition to the other symptoms of endometriosis.

Rectal and Bladder Involvement. When endometrial implants invade the small intestine or colon, unpleasant symptoms may result. Endometrial implants that invade the bowel can cause constipation, painful bowel movements, and rectal bleeding. Since hemorrhoids or even cancer can cause similar symptoms, all symptoms that might be caused by bowel invasion need to be carefully evaluated by a physician. Invasion of the small intestine by endometriosis can cause abdominal swelling, pain, and vomiting.

Occasionally, endometriosis will invade the bladder and cause symptoms similar to urinary tract infections with urinary frequency, pain on urination, urinary retention, and blood in the urine during menstruation.

Endometrial Cysts. These cysts, also called "chocolate cysts," tend to be deep brown in color, and are filled with old blood and endometrial cells. They can vary greatly in size, ranging from quite small to larger than a grapefruit. They tend to grow fast and even leak blood, which causes much pain. They can also rupture and present with symptoms much like acute appendicitis, a surgical emergency.

In summary, symptoms such as menstrual cramps and pain, pain on sexual intercourse, infertility, abnormal bleeding, blood and bladder symptoms, and endometrial cysts can be seen in varying degrees in women with endometriosis. How severe the symptoms are depend on the site of the implants and determine how aggressive the medical treatment needs to be to help relieve the symptoms and control the underlying process of endometriosis.

DIAGNOSIS OF ENDOMETRIOSIS

Physical signs of endometriosis can be noted during a pelvis exam by a gynecologist. Often, the uterus is fixed and not freely mobile; it can also be retroverted, or tilted backward. Endometrial, or chocolate cysts, may be large and easy to feel. Patients may complain of pelvic tenderness during the examination because of endometrial implants located in the pelvis region. Endometrial implants located in the uterosacral ligaments will feel nodular and shotty (hard and round, like a shot pellet) on examination. Tenderness is particularly noted at the time of menstruation.

For a definitive diagnosis of endometriosis, a laparoscopy is usually necessary. The laparoscope is a visualization device shaped like a thin tube. The device is inserted through a small abdominal incision. Gas is introduced into the abdomen to move the organs apart for better visualization of any disease process. This also allows the physician to see the ovaries and fallopian tubes. Laparoscopy enables the physician to see any lesions that have the typical appearance of endometriosis implants; it can also be used to determine if fertilization is impaired by the implants. This is important for women who wish to become pregnant and for whom possible infertility caused by endometriosis is an issue.

Surgical treatment can usually be initiated at the time of laparoscopy. Adhesions and implants can be dissolved with a laser or by electrocauterization. However, there are women with endometriosis for whom laparoscopy is not advisable. These include patients with extensive endometriosis, massive scarring, or implants that have invaded deep into the ovaries, urinary tract, or bowels. These patients will often require more extensive surgery.

Other imaging techniques may give additional clues to the locations of the endometrial implants. Ultrasound is a noninvasive technique that allows visualization of pelvic structures such as the uterus and ovaries by bouncing high-frequency sound waves off these solid masses. The waves bounce back in patterns that appear as pictures on a screen. The technique is particularly helpful in diagnosing chocolate ovarian cysts and fibroid tumors. In women with symptoms such as urinary frequency, blood in the urine at menstruation, and bladder pain, all of which suggest endometrial invasion of the bladder wall, specific X-rays of the genitourinary tract may be necessary.

There are a variety of techniques that can help the physician differentiate endometriosis from menstrual cramps, ovarian cysts, pelvic infections, and a host of other symptoms. With accurate diagnosis of the exact locations of the implants, therapy can be targeted most effectively in the effort to combat this difficult disease.

EVALUATE YOUR RISK FACTORS

An important part of your self-help program is your personal evaluation of the fibroid or endometriosis problem for which you are seeking solutions. The risk factor and lifestyle evaluations will help you assess specific areas of your life—diet, exercise, stress—to see which of your habit patterns may be contributing to your health problems. I have found that lifestyle habits significantly affect the symptoms of fibroids and endometriosis. When you've completed these evaluations, you will be ready to go on to the self-help chapters that follow and begin planning and initiating your personal treatment program.

You are at higher risk of developing fibroids or endometriosis and suffering from symptoms caused by either of these problems if you have any of the following risk factors. Check each factor that applies to you.

Risk Factors
Career or working woman   —
High-stress life, combining work and child care   —
Age twenties through forties   —
Childlessness (endometriosis)   —

Multiple pregnancies (fibroids) —
Tendency toward ovarian cysts that bleed —
(endometriosis)
Mothers or sisters with a history of endometriosis —
or fibroids
High levels of estrogen as determined by your —
physician, or use of estrogen-containing
medication
High levels of prostaglandin hormones as deter- —
mined by your physician
Repeated laparoscopies —
Significant life stress —
Emotional distress that hampers well-being, anxi- —
ety, depression
Concurrent immune stress, recurrent or chronic in- —
fections, allergies
High dietary intake of meat, saturated fat, dairy —
products, alcohol, sugar, caffeine, salt, or
chocolate
Lack of B vitamins —
Lack of exercise —

EATING HABITS

All the foods in the following list are high-stress foods that can worsen the symptoms of both fibroids and endometriosis. If you eat many of these foods, or if you eat any of these foods frequently, your nutritional habits may be contributing significantly to your symptoms.

Whole grains, vegetables, fruit and fish are high-nutrient, low-stress foods that may help to relieve or prevent fibroid and endometriosis symptoms. Include these foods frequently in your diet. If you are already eating many of these foods and few of the high-stress foods, chances are your nutritional habits are good, and food selection may not be a significant factor in worsening your fibroids or endometriosis. You may want to look carefully at the stress management and exercise chapters. The activities contained in these chapters may be very helpful in relieving your symptoms.

Foods That Increase Symptoms

- Cow's milk
- Cow's cheese
- Butter
- Yogurt
- Eggs
- Chocolate
- Sugar
- Alcohol
- Wheat bread
- Wheat noodles
- Wheat-based flour
- Pastries
- Added salt
- Bouillon
- Commercial salad dressing
- Catsup
- Coffee
- Black tea
- Soft drinks
- Hot dogs
- Ham
- Bacon
- Beef
- Lamb
- Pork

Foods That Decrease Symptoms

- All fruits and vegetables
- Whole grains such as brown rice, oatmeal and millet
- Raw nuts and seeds
- Fish
- Chicken or turkey with skin removed
- Vegetable oils such as flax seed oil and olive oil

EXERCISE HABITS

Exercise helps prevent the pain and cramps related to fibroids and endometriosis by relaxing muscles and promoting better blood circulation and oxygenation to the pelvic area. Exercise can also help reduce stress and relieve anxiety and upset. If your total number of exercise periods per week is less than three, you will probably be prone to pain and cramp symptoms.

If you are exercising more than three times a week, keep doing your exercises; they are probably making your symptoms less severe. You may want to add specific corrective exercises to your present regime, choosing them to fit your individual symptoms.

Beneficial Exercises

- Walking
- Running
- Dancing
- Swimming
- Bicycling
- Tennis
- Stretching
- Yoga

The Role of Stress

The following evaluation is a very important one for women with fibroids or endometriosis. Not all stresses have a major impact on our lives, as do death, divorce, or personal injury. Most of us are exposed to a multitude of small life stresses on a daily basis. The effects of these stresses are cumulative and can be a major factor in worsening fibroid- or endometriosis-related muscle tension and pain in the pelvic area. After completing the checklist, read over the day-to-day stress areas that you find difficult to handle. Becoming aware of them is the first step toward lessening their effects on your life.

Check each item that seems to apply to you.

Work

___ **Too much responsibility.** You feel there are too many demands made of you.

___ **Time urgency.** You always feel rushed.

___ **Job instability.** You are concerned about losing your job.

___ **Job performance.** You don't feel that you are working up to your maximum capability.

___ **Difficulty getting along with co-workers and boss.**

___ **Understimulation.** Work is boring.

___ **Uncomfortable physical plant.** Lights are too bright or too dim; noises are loud. You're exposed to noxious fumes or chemicals.

Spouse or Significant Other

— **Hostile communication.** There is too much negative emotion and drama.
— **Not enough communication.** You feel that an emotional bond is lacking between you.
— **Discrepancy in communication.** One person talks about feelings too much, the other person too little.
— **Affection.** You do not feel you receive enough affection, or you are made uncomfortable by your partner's demands.
— **Sexuality.** You feel deprived by your partner or your partner demands sexual relations too often.
— **Children.** They make too many demands on your time. They are hard to discipline.
— **Organization.** Home is poorly organized. It always seems messy; chores are half-finished.
— **Time.** There is too much to do in the home and never enough time to get it all done.
— **Responsibility.** You need more help.

Your Emotional State

— **Too much anxiety.** You worry too much about every little thing.
— **Victimization.** You feel everyone is taking advantage of you.
— **Poor self-image.** You are always finding fault with yourself.
— **Too critical.** You are always finding fault with others.
— **Inability to relax.**
— **Not enough self-renewal.** You don't take enough time off to relax and have fun.
— **Feeling of depression.** You feel blue, isolated, and tired.
— **Too angry.** Small life issues seem to upset you unduly.

FINDING THE SOLUTIONS

How Diet Can Help

I cannot emphasize too strongly the importance of good dietary habits for women beginning a fibroid and endometriosis treatment program. After years of working with thousands of women patients, including many with these problems, I have found that no therapy can be fully effective without including beneficial dietary changes as part of the treatment plan. The best therapeutic program can be subverted by a diet full of saturated fat, sugar, salt, caffeine, alcohol, and other high-stress food items. While many of these ingredients are found in the commonly eaten American "fast foods" and "junk foods," they are also found in foods that are considered staples.

Many women eat a diet they mistakenly think is healthy, not realizing that their food selection is actually worsening their symptoms. Luckily, the list of foods that help relieve and prevent fibroids and endometriosis is a long one. Once you shift to a diet of these more healthful foods, you will find that they are just as delicious, convenient, and easy to prepare as the foods you are eating now.

I discuss in this chapter both the foods to avoid and foods to emphasize for fibroids and endometriosis relief. The information on these foods is the result of almost two decades of work with women who have come to me with these problems and have had significant relief of their symptoms. I have been very impressed by how many women with fibroids and endometriosis have reported a noticeable decrease in heavy bleeding as well as pain and discomfort level within one or two menstrual cycles after starting my program. Besides the specific benefits these dietary principles will have on your cramps, they will also aid your general health and well-being. Many women have reported that they have more energy and a greater sense of well-being than they have had in years. Often they tell me that symptoms they never associated with their menstrual bleeding and cramps, such as allergies and generally poor digestive function, have cleared up as well.

Foods to Emphasize

You should emphasize the following foods in your diet. They will provide the range of nutrients that you need to help balance your hormones, reduce your estrogen levels, decrease cramping and inflammation, and generally improve your physical and mental well-being. Even though fibroid and endometriosis symptoms are worse during the second half of the menstrual cycle, these healthful foods should form the mainstay of your diet throughout the entire month. A poorly chosen high-stress diet during your symptom-free time will increase the severity of your symptoms when menstruation starts.

Whole Grains. I strongly recommend the use of certain whole grains such as millet, buckwheat, oats, and rice. Many women also tolerate 100% rye well. Whole grains are excellent sources of vitamin B and vitamin E, both of which are critical for healthy hormonal balance and lowering excessive estrogen levels through their beneficial effect on both the liver and ovaries. The vitamin B and vitamin E content of whole grains also help combat the fatigue and depression that is often seen with the onset of menstruation.

Grains are excellent sources of magnesium, which helps reduce neuromuscular tension and thereby decreases menstrual cramps. They are also fairly high in calcium, which relaxes muscle contraction. In addition, they are excellent sources of potassium. Potassium has a diuretic effect on the body tissues and helps reduce bloating. Excessive fluid retention is one of the main causes of the congestive symptoms seen with cramps that are characterized by dull, aching pain.

While many whole grains are beneficial, women with severe fibroid and endometriosis symptoms may need to avoid whole wheat and even try a wheat-free diet. This probably comes as a surprise to you because wheat is a mainstay of the American diet. However, wheat contains a protein called gluten that is difficult to digest and can be highly allergenic. In a number of women patients who had fibroids or endometriosis coexisting with PMS symptoms, I have seen wheat worsen their fatigue, depression, bloating, constipation, diarrhea, and intestinal cramps. You may want to try a wheat-free diet to see if you feel better once wheat is eliminated. If you have more severe gluten intolerance or food allergies, you may want to eliminate oats and rye also, since they contain some gluten as well. You may find that you feel best eating buckwheat, corn, and rice. Even these grains should be rotated and used carefully by women who have food allergies and menstrual cramps.

Whole grains provide other benefits to fibroid or endometriosis sufferers; they are excellent sources of protein, especially when combined with beans and peas. I strongly recommend vegetable sources of protein for women with these two problems, since such proteins are easily digestible. In addition, the fiber in whole grains absorbs estrogen and helps remove it from the body through bowel elimination. Fiber can also help decrease the congestive symptoms of cramps since it produces bulkier stools with a higher water content. This helps to eliminate excessive fluid from the body.

Fiber may also be helpful in reducing the digestive symptoms that occur with fibroids or endometriosis. It has a normalizing effect on the bowel movements, helping to eliminate both constipation and diarrhea. Besides removing excessive estrogen and water from the body, whole grains help to bind dietary fat and eliminate it from the body as well as help to lower cholesterol. Oat and rice bran are particularly good for this purpose. Because cancers of the breast, uterus, ovaries, and colon are linked to a diet high in animal fats, the use of whole grains may have a protective effect in preventing the development of these diseases.

Legumes. Beans and peas are excellent sources of calcium, magnesium, and potassium. Particularly good choices include tofu, black beans, pinto beans, kidney beans, chickpeas, lentils, lima beans, and soybeans. These foods are also high in iron and tend to be good sources of copper and zinc; women with fibroids and endometriosis who suffer from heavy bleeding are often deficient in these minerals, particularly iron. Legumes are very high in vitamin B complex and vitamin B_6, necessary nutrients for healthy liver function, reducing excess estrogen levels, and preventing cramps and menstrual fatigue. They are also excellent sources of protein and can be used as substitutes for meat at many meals; legumes provide all the essential amino acids when eaten with grains. Good examples of grain and legume combinations include meals such as beans and rice, or corn bread and split pea soup.

Like grains, legumes, are a good source of fiber and can help normalize bowel function and lower cholesterol. They digest slowly and can help to regulate the blood sugar level, a trait they share with whole grains. As a result, they are an excellent food for women with diabetes or blood sugar imbalances. Some women find that gas is a problem when they eat beans. You can minimize gas by using digestive enzymes and eating beans in small quantities.

Vegetables. These are outstanding foods for relief of fibroid and endometriosis symptoms of all types. Many vegetables are high in calcium, magnesium, and potassium, which help to relieve and prevent the spasmodic symptoms of cramps. Besides helping relax tense, irritable muscles, these minerals help calm and relax the emotions, too. Both calcium and magnesium act as natural tranquilizers, a real benefit for women suffering from menstrual pain, discomfort, and irritability. The potassium content of vegetables helps to relieve the symptoms of menstrual congestion by reducing fluid retention and bloating. Some of the best sources for these minerals include Swiss chard, spinach, broccoli, beet greens, mustard greens, sweet potatoes, kale, potatoes, green peas, and green beans. These vegetables are also high in iron, which may help reduce bleeding and cramps.

Many vegetables are high in vitamin C, which helps decrease capillary fragility and facilitate the flow of essential nutrients into the tight muscles as well as the flow of waste products out. Decreased capillary fragility also means a reduction in the heavy menstrual bleeding commonly seen with fibroids and endometriosis. Vitamin C is an important antistress vitamin because it is needed for healthy adrenal hormonal production (the adrenals are important glands that help the body deal with stress). Vitamin C is also important for immune function and wound healing. Because of these properties, vitamin C may help limit the scarring and inflammation caused in the pelvis by the endometrial implants. Its anti-infectious properties may reduce the tendency toward bladder and vaginal infections. Vegetables high in vitamin C include brussels sprouts, broccoli, cauliflower, kale, peppers, parsley, peas, tomatoes, and potatoes.

Fruits. Fruits also contain a wide range of nutrients that can benefit menstrual cramps. Like many vegetables, fruits are an excellent source of vitamin C and bioflavonoids. Both of these nutrients prevent capillary fragility and reduce heavy menstrual flow. By strengthening blood vessels, they promote good blood circulation into the tense pelvic muscles. Almost all fruits contain some vitamin C, with the best sources being berries, oranges, grapefruits, and melons. These fruits are also good sources of bioflavonoids.

Bioflavonoids, interestingly enough, are also weakly estrogenic and antiestrogenic. This was first discovered many years ago when sheep grazing on certain types of clover showed estrogenic stimulation of the uterus. When analyzed chemically, however, these natural plant estrogens were found to be only 1/50,000 as potent as the levels used in drugs. Though bioflavonoids are weakly estrogenic themselves, they interfere with the production of estrogen by competing with estrogen precursors for binding sites on enzymes. Thus, bioflavonoids help to normalize the body's estrogen levels. They help elevate estrogen levels when they are too low, as in menopausal women, and help bring down excessive estrogen levels when they are too high, as may occur in women with fibroids and endometriosis.

Certain fruits are also excellent sources of calcium and magnesium; you can eat them often for your mineral needs. These include dried figs, raisins, blackberries, bananas, and oranges. Figs, raisins, and bananas are also exceptional sources of potassium, so should be eaten by women with fatigue and bloating. All fruits, in fact, are an excellent source of potassium. Eat fruits whole to take advantage of their high fiber content. This fiber content helps prevent constipation and the other digestive irregularities frequently seen with menstrual pain and cramps.

Fresh and dried fruits are excellent snack and dessert substitutes for cookies, candies, cakes, and other foods high in refined sugar. Though fruit is high in sugar, its high fiber content slows down absorption of the sugar into the blood circulation and helps stabilize the blood sugar level. I recommend, however, using fruit juices only in small quantities. Fruit juice does not contain the bulk or fiber of the whole fruit. As a result, it acts more like table sugar and can dramatically destabilize your blood sugar level when used in excess. In this case, less is better. If you want fruit juice on a more frequent basis, mix it half-and-half with water.

Seeds and Nuts. Seeds and nuts are the best sources of the two essential fatty acids, linoleic acid and linolenic acid. These acids provide the raw materials your body needs to produce the muscle-relaxant prostaglandin hormones. Adequate levels of essential fatty acids in your diet are very important in treating and preventing endometriosis-related muscle cramps and inflammation. The best sources of both fatty acids are raw flax and pumpkin seeds. Sesame and sunflower seeds are excellent sources of linoleic acid alone. Seeds and nuts are also very high in other essential nutrients that women need, such as magnesium, calcium, and potassium. Particularly good to eat are sesame seeds, sunflower seeds, pistachios, pecans, and almonds. Because they are very high in calories, seeds and nuts should be eaten in small amounts.

The oils in seeds and nuts are very perishable, so avoid exposure to light, heat, and oxygen. Seeds and nuts should be eaten raw and unsalted to get the benefit of their essential fatty acids (which are good for your skin and hair) as well as to avoid the negative effects of too much salt. Shell them yourself, when possible. If you buy them already shelled, refrigerate them so their oils don't become rancid. They are a wonderful garnish on salads, vegetable dishes, and casseroles. They can also be eaten as a main source of protein in snacks and light meals.

Meat, Poultry, and Fish. I generally recommend eating meat only in small quantities or avoiding it altogether if you have fibroid and endometriosis symptoms. Beef, pork, lamb, and poultry contain saturated fats that produce the muscle-contracting F_2 Alpha prostaglandins. These hormones trigger muscle contraction and constriction in blood vessels, as well as inflammation, thereby worsening endometriosis-related cramps and the spread of endometrial implants.

If you do eat meat, I recommend emphasizing fish or poultry (without the skin). Fish, unlike other meat, contains linolenic acid, one of the fatty acids that help to relax muscles through the beneficial prostaglandin pathway—specifically, the series-one and series-three prostaglandins. Fish are also excellent sources of minerals, especially iodine and potassium. Particularly good types of fish for women with menstrual cramps are salmon, tuna, mackerel, and trout. Poultry also contains essential fatty acids, but to a lesser degress than fish.

If you include meat, I recommend using it in very small amounts (3 ounces or less per day). Most Americans eat much more protein than is healthy. Excessive amounts of protein are difficult to digest and stress the kidneys. Except for fish, meat is also a main source of unhealthy saturated fats, which put you at higher risk of heart disease and cancer. Instead of using meat as your only source of protein, I recommend that you increase your intake of grains, beans, raw seeds, and nuts, which contain protein as well as many other important nutrients. I also recommend buying the meat of organic, range-fed animals; this reduces the exposure to pesticides, antibiotics, and hormones.

Oils. You can use vegetable oils in small amounts for cooking, stir-frying, and sautéing. When you do, select an oil like corn oil that contains vitamin E. Vitamin E is an important nutrient in reducing the mood symptoms, fatigue, and cramps that occur at the onset of menstruation for women whose fibroids or endometriosis coexists with PMS.

Vitamin E may help regulate hormone levels. This is important because high levels of estrogen stimulate the growth of fibroids and endometriosis. Women with these problems should use vitamin E in supplemental form. Other good oils for cooking are olive oil and canola oil.

Flax oil, which is notable for its beautiful golden color and delicious nutty flavor, can be used to enhance the flavor of rice, steamed vegetables, toast, popcorn, and many other foods. Many of my patients use it as a butter substitute. However, you cannot cook with flax oil because it is very perishable, sensitive to heat, light, and oxygen. Instead, you must first cook the food, then add the flax oil just before serving. Keep flax oil tightly capped and refrigerated. All oils should be cold-pressed to help ensure freshness and purity. Keep your oils refrigerated to avoid rancidity.

Foods to Avoid

If you have fibroids or endometriosis, you should avoid or use only limited amounts of the foods described in this section, because they can worsen your monthly symptoms.

Dairy Products. Dairy products should be avoided by women with fibroids or endometriosis. This is always a surprise to women, because dairy products have traditionally been touted as one of the four basic food groups. Many women use them as staples in their diets, eating large amounts of cheese, yogurt, milk, and cottage cheese. Yet, dairy products are the main dietary source of arachidonic acid, the fat used by your body to product muscle-contracting F_2 Alpha prostaglandins. These prostaglandins can worsen the pelvic pain, cramps, and inflammation characteristic or endometriosis. By deleting all dairy products from the diet, the severity of menstrual pain and cramps can be decreased by as much as one-third to one-half within one to two menstrual cycles.

The high saturated-fat content of many dairy products is a risk factor for excess estrogen levels in the body. Excessive estrogen is a trigger for fibroids and endometriosis and accelerates the spread of the disease. High estrogen levels have also been linked to heavy menstrual bleeding, another common complaint of women with these problems. Excessive estrogen can also worsen fibrocystic breast disease. The high salt content of dairy products worsens the bloating and fluid retention of congestive dysmenorrhea, too.

Dairy products have many other unhealthy effects on a woman's body. The tryptophan in milk has a sedative effect that increases fatigue, a real problem for some women the first day or two of their periods. Many people are allergic to dairy products or lack the enzymes to digest milk. The result can be digestive problems such as bloating, gas, and bowel changes, which intensify with menstruation. This intolerance to dairy products can hamper the absorption and assimilation of their calcium. Dairy products have also been shown in clinical studies to decrease iron absorption in anemic women.

Because dairy products are a risk factor for fibroids and endometriosis, women who have depended on dairy products for their calcium intake naturally wonder about alternative sources. The many other good dietary sources of this essential nutrient include beans, peas, soybeans, sesame seeds, soup stock made from chicken or fish bones, and green leafy vegetables. For food preparation, soy milk, potato milk, and nut milk are excellent substitutes. You can also use a supplement containing calcium, magnesium, and vitamin D to make sure your intake is sufficient. Nondairy milks are available at health food stores and some supermarkets.

Fats. Saturated fats in general come from animal sources, and from a few vegetable sources such as palm oil or coconut oil. Like dairy products, they contain arachidonic acid, and therefore can intensify menstrual cramps by stimulating production of the muscle-contracting prostaglandins. A diet full of dairy products, red meat, and eggs promotes heavy menstrual bleeding and even fibroid tumor growth in susceptible women. Excessive saturated fat intake is stressful to the liver, so the liver is less able to break down estrogen efficiently, leading to excess estrogen levels. Fibroids can worsen cramps when they grow to be too large, cutting off their own blood supply and pressing on the bladder and intestines.

Salt. Excessive salt intake can worsen the menstrual symptoms that frequently occur in women with fibroids and endometriosis. Too much dietary salt can increase bloating and fluid retention, particularly in women who have coexisting PMS. Too much salt intake can also increase high blood pressure and is a risk factor in the development of osteoporosis in menopausal women. Unfortunately, most processed food contains large amounts of salt. Frozen and canned foods are often loaded with salt. Fast foods such as hamburgers, hot dogs, french fries, pizza, and tacos are loaded with salt and saturated fats.

Women with fibroids and endometriosis should avoid adding salt to their meals. For flavor, use seasonings like garlic, herbs, spices, and lemon juice. Avoid processed foods that are high in salt, such as canned foods, olives, pickles, potato chips, tortilla chips, catsup, and salad dressings. Learn to read labels and look for the word sodium (salt). If it appears high on the list of ingredients, don't buy the product. Many items in health food stores are labeled "no salt added." Some supermarkets also offer "no added salt" foods in their diet or health food sections.

Alcohol. Women with fibroids or endometriosis should avoid alcohol entirely or consume it only in small amounts. Like dairy products and saturated fats, alcohol is stressful to the liver and can affect the liver's ability to metabolize hormones efficiently. Excessive alcohol intake has been associated with both lack of ovulation and elevated estrogen levels, which can trigger the growth and spread of endometrial implants in susceptible women, worsening menstrual cramps and pain. It can also trigger heavy bleeding in estrogen-sensitive women with fibroids and endometriosis. Excessive estrogen can worsen the congestive symptoms of menstrual pain and cramps. Estrogen causes fluid and salt retention in the body. When levels are too high, the body can retain excessive amounts of fluid during the premenstrual and menstrual phases of the month.

Alcohol also depletes the body's B-complex vitamins and minerals such as magnesium by disrupting carbohydrate metabolism. Because minerals are important in regulating muscle tension, an alcohol-based nutritional deficiency can worsen muscle spasms at the time of menstruation. Depletion of magnesium and vitamin B complex can also intensify menstrual fatigue and mood swings.

Though alcohol has a relaxing effect and can enhance the taste of food, I recommend that women with fibroids or endometriosis avoid or limit its use, particularly in the early stages of treatment. This is even more important for women who have coexisting PMS. For these women, the use of alcohol can aggravate the PMS-related mood swings, irritability, and other symptoms.

If you entertain a great deal and enjoy social drinking, try using nonalcoholic beverages. A nonalcoholic cocktail such as mineral water with a twist of lime or lemon or a dash of bitters is a good substitute. "Near beer" is a nonalcoholic beer substitute that tastes quite good. Light wine and beer—in small amounts—have a lower alcohol content than hard liquor, liqueurs, and regular wine.

Sugar. Like alcohol, sugar depletes the body's B-complex vitamins and minerals, which can worsen muscle tension and irritability as well as nervous tension and anxiety. Lack of certain B vitamins also hampers the liver's ability to handle fats, including the fat-based hormone estrogen. One particular B vitamin, B_6, is also needed for the production of beneficial types of prostaglandins that have relaxant and anti-inflammatory effects, both important for the treatment of endometriosis.

Unfortunately, sugar addiction is very common in our society in people of all ages. Many people use sweet foods as a way to deal with their frustrations and other upsets. As a result, most Americans eat too much sugar—the average American eats 120 pounds each year. Many convenience foods, such as salad dressing, catsup, and relish, contain high levels of both sugar and salt. Sugar is the main ingredient in soft drinks and in desserts such as candies, cookies, cakes, and ice cream.

Try to satisfy your sweet tooth instead with healthier foods, such as fruit or grain-based desserts like oatmeal cookies made with fruit or honey. You will find that small amounts of these foods can satisfy your cravings.

Caffeine. Coffee, black tea, soft drinks, and chocolate—all these foods contain caffeine, a stimulant that many women use to increase their energy level and alertness and decrease fatigue. Caffeine is even used in many over-the-counter menstrual remedies that women with early-stage endometriosis often take for symptom relief. Unfortunately, caffeine has many negative effects on the body. For example, caffeine used in excess increases anxiety, irritability, and mood swings. This can be a real problem for women in whom PMS coexists with fibroids or endometriosis. Caffeine also depletes the body's stores of B-complex vitamins and essential minerals, so long-term use can increase fibroid- and endometriosis-related pain, cramps, and bleeding by disrupting both carbohydrate metabolism and healthy liver function. Many menopausal women also complain that caffeine increases the number of hot flashes. Coffee, black tea, chocolate, and caffeinated soft drinks all act to inhibit iron absorption, thus worsening anemia.

VITAMINS, MINERALS, HERBS & ESSENTIAL FATTY ACIDS

Nutritional supplements can play an important role in the treatment and prevention of fibroids and endometriosis. Supplements can help to balance hormones and reduce estrogen levels. When used properly, they can have a dramatic effect on the regulation of bleeding and the reduction of the pain and cramps that may accompany both fibroids and endometriosis. The importance of nutrition in balancing estrogen levels and relieving excessive menstrual bleeding, cramping, and pain is supported by many medical research studies done at university centers and hospitals.

Use of supplements must go hand in hand with a low-stress, healthful diet. It is not enough to take supplements and continue with poor dietary habits. I have seen women try this and not get the results they're looking for. However, diet alone can't provide the nutrient levels necessary for optimal healing. The use of supplements can speed up and facilitate the return to vibrant health and well-being.

Vitamins and Minerals

The following vitamins and minerals play an important role in both the symptomatic relief and prevention of fibroids and endometriosis.

Vitamin A. Heavy menstrual bleeding is a significant problem for women with fibroids and is the most common reason for hysterectomies. Bleeding is also a significant problem for women with endometriosis. Fortunately, vitamin A can play a role in reducing these symptoms.

There are two types of vitamin A. Vitamin A from animal sources usually comes from fish liver and is oil soluble. This type of vitamin A can be toxic if taken in too large a dose (i.e., greater than 25,000 international units [I.U.] per day, if taken for more than a few months). In contrast, beta carotene, the precursor of vitamin A found in plants, is water soluble and is not toxic in large amounts. A single sweet potato or cup of carrot juice contains more than 20,000 I.U. of beta carotene.

Vitamin B Complex. The vitamin B complex consists of eleven factors that perform many important biochemical functions in the body. These include stabilization of brain chemistry, glucose metabolism, and the inactivation of estrogen by the liver. Since fibroids and endometriosis can be triggered by excess estrogen in the body, it is important that estrogen levels are properly regulated through breakdown and disposal by the liver.

Besides helping to regulate estrogen levels, B vitamins have been found useful for the reduction of menstrual pain and cramps, particularly vitamin B_6 or pyridoxine. In clinical studies, use of B_6 led to a reduction in PMS-related cramping, fluid retention, weight gain, and fatigue. PMS often co-exists with fibroids and endometriosis.

Vitamin B_6 is also an important factor in the conversion of linoleic acid to gamma linolenic acid (GLA) in the production of the beneficial series-one prostaglandins. Series-one prostaglandins have a relaxant effect on uterine muscles as well as anti-inflammatory effect on various tissues. As a result they can help relieve cramps, reduce symptoms of endo-metriosis, and possibly help limit the spread of implants. Because vitamin B_6 levels drop in women using the birth control pill, a common treatment for both spasmodic dys-menorrhea and endometriosis, these women should take supplemental B_6. Such women safely take B_6 in doses up to 300 milligrams. Avoid doses above this level because they can be neurotoxic.

For women with fibroids and endometriosis, I generally recommend 50 to 100 milligrams per day of vitamin B com-plex, with additional B_6 (up to 300 milligrams total daily dose), if appropriate. The B vitamins are water soluble and easily lost from the body. In fact, emotional and nutritional stress accelerate the loss of these essential nutrients. This can worsen symptoms seen with fibroids and endometriosis, including fatigue, faintness, and dizziness. Even with sup-plementation, a diet high in B complex is desirable for all women. The B-complex vitamins are commonly found in whole grains, beans and peas, and liver.

Vitamin C. Vitamin C has been tested, along with biofla-vonoids, as a treatment for heavy menstrual bleeding, which is commonly found in women with fibroids and endometrio-sis. Vitamin C helps reduce bleeding by strengthening capil-laries and preventing capillary fragility. Women who bleed excessively may eventually become iron deficient and end up with anemia. Vitamin C helps increase iron absorption from food sources such as bran, peas, seeds, nuts, and leafy green vegetables. This can help prevent iron deficiency ane-mia in women with heavy bleeding.

Vitamin C also helps decrease menstrual cramps and pain by permitting better flow of nutrients into the tight and con-tracted uterine muscle. It also facilitates the flow of waste products out of the uterus, ensuring that waste products that worsen cramping and pain, like lactic acid and carbon diox-ide, are more efficiently released from the pelvic region. Vi-tamin C is an important antistress vitamin essential for healthy adrenal function and immune function. It may help to limit the spread of endometrial implants through stimu-lating immune function and limiting inflammation and scarring. Vitamin C can also help decrease the fatigue and lethargy symptoms that accompany cramps.

I recommend that women with excessive bleeding and cramps use between 1000 to 4000 milligrams of vitamin C per day, especially when symptoms occur. Many fruits and vegetables are excellent sources of vitamin C.

Bioflavonoids. Like vitamin C, bioflavonoids have also shown dramatic results in their ability to reduce heavy menstrual bleeding through strengthening the capillary walls; they have been studied in conjunction with vitamin C for relief of bleeding. Bioflavonoids have been used in women with bleeding due to hormonal imbalance and have been tested in women who have lost multiple pregnancies due to bleeding. In nature, bioflavonoids can often be found with vitamin C in fruits and vegetables. For example, they are found in grape skins, cherries, blackberries, and blueberries. Bioflavonoids are also abundant in citrus fruits, especially in the pulp and the white rind. They are also found in buckwheat and soybeans.

Bioflavonoids have the additional property of being weakly estrogenic and antiestrogenic, important properties for control of fibroid and endometriosis symptoms. These estrogen-like chemicals (called phytoestrogens) have a similar chemical structure and activity to the estrogen that your body produces. However, although these plants are estrogenic, the doses they contain are much weaker than the levels in drugs. (Bioflavonoids contain 1/50,000 the potency of a drug dose of estrogen.) Also, plant sources of estrogen can compete with estrogen precursors produced by your body for space on the binding sites of enzymes needed for estrogen production. Thus, on the one hand, bioflavonoids can act to lower estrogen levels in the body for women with fibroids and endometriosis whose symptoms are triggered by excessive estrogen. On the other hand, the weakly estrogenic effect of the bioflavonoids can help relieve symptoms such as hot flashes, night sweats, and mood swings in menopausal women who are grossly deficient in estrogen.

Vitamin E. Like bioflavonoids, this essential nutrient has been used to relieve symptoms triggered by excessive estrogen levels, including PMS, fibrocystic breast disease, and breast tenderness. I have found vitamin E to be a useful part of a therapeutic program in women with heavy menstrual bleeding due to fibroids and endometriosis.

Vitamin E has also been tested in clinical studies as a treatment for menstrual cramps and pain. Taken in doses of 150 I.U. ten days premenstrual and during the first four days of the menstrual period, it helped to relieve symptoms of menstrual discomfort in approximately 70 percent of the women tested within two menstrual cycles.

The best natural sources of vitamin E are wheat germ oil, walnut oil, soybean oil, and other grain and seed oil sources. I generally recommend that women with fibroids and endometriosis use between 400 and 2000 I.U. per day. Women with hypertension and diabetes should start on a much lower dose of vitamin E (100 I.U. per day). Any increase in dosage should be made slowly and monitored carefully in these women. Otherwise, vitamin E tends to be extremely safe and is commonly used by millions of people.

Iron. Women who suffer from heavy menstrual bleeding due to fibroids and endometriosis tend to be iron deficient. In fact, some medical studies have found that inadequate iron intake may even cause excessive bleeding. Women who suffer from heavy menstrual bleeding should have their red blood count checked to see if they need supplemental iron in addition to a high iron-content diet. Heme iron, the iron from meat sources like liver, is much better absorbed and assimilated than nonheme iron, the iron from vegetarian sources. To be absorbed properly, nonheme iron must be taken with at least 75 milligrams of vitamin C.

Iron deficiency is the main cause of anemia due to heavy menstrual flow. Good food sources of iron include liver, blackstrap molasses, beans and peas, seeds and nuts, and certain fruits and vegetables.

Calcium. This important mineral helps to prevent menstrual pain and cramps by maintaining normal muscle tone. Because cramps are common with fibroids and endometriosis, calcium intake is important to help prevent further muscular irritability. When taken before bed at night, calcium is effective in helping to combat insomnia due to menstrual discomfort. Muscles that are calcium deficient tend to be hyperactive and more likely to cramp. Since the uterus is made up of muscle, it is susceptible to calcium deficiency. Besides promoting normal muscle tone and activity, calcium is a major structural component of bone.

Unfortunately, calcium deficiency is common in our society. The recommended daily allowance (RDA) for calcium in menstruating women is 800 milligrams per day and rises to as much as 1500 milligrams per day in postmenopausal women. The typical American diet supplies only about 450 to 550 milligrams per day. No wonder so many American women are at risk for problems like menstrual cramps and osteoporosis. Good food sources of calcium include green leafy vegetables, beans and peas, seeds and nuts, blackstrap molasses, and seafood.

Magnesium. Magnesium has an important effect on the neuromuscular system in reducing menstrual cramps. A deficiency of magnesium increases muscular hyperactivity and can worsen menstrual pain that is already severe due to fibroids and endometriosis. Magnesium optimizes the amount of usable calcium in your system by increasing calcium absorption. Conversely, calcium can interfere with magnesium absorption. Magnesium deficiency contributes to menstrual fatigue, dizziness, and fainting because of its importance in glucose metabolism. A magnesium deficiency can hinder the normal conversion of food to usable energy. Magnesium is also needed for the conversion of linoleic acid to gamma linolenic acid (GLA), and a deficiency of magnesium retards the conversion of essential fatty acids to the series-one prostaglandins. Like calcium, magnesium is an important structural component of healthy bone tissue, necessary for the prevention of osteoporosis. It is usually recommended that the diet include half as much magnesium as calcium, or approximately 400 milligrams per day.

Potassium. Potassium is the third mineral, along with calcium and magnesium, that helps reduce cramps by regulating muscle contraction. Thus, adequate levels of potassium in the body are necessary to prevent worsening of menstrual cramps. Women deficient in potassium may suffer from premenstrual uterine cramping, leg cramps, and even irregular heartbeats. Potassium also plays a role in the maintenance of fluid balance and energy levels. Women low in potassium are more prone to PMS-related bloating, fatigue, and weakness. Women suffering from endometriosis-related diarrhea may lose significant amounts of potassium through watery bowel movements.

For women suffering from these symptoms, the use of a potassium supplement may be helpful. The most common dose available is a 99-milligram tablet or capsule. I generally recommend taking one to three per day for up to one week premenstrually. Potassium, however, must be used cautiously. It should be avoided by women with kidney or cardiovascular disease, because a high level of potassium can cause an irregular heartbeat in women with these problems. Also, potassium can be irritating to the intestinal tract, so it should be taken with meals.

Herbs

A wide variety of herbs can help alleviate symptoms of fibroids and endometriosis. I have used many of these herbs in my practice for years and have found them to be gentle, effective remedies for many women. Some herbs have a hormone-balancing effect and help lower excessive estrogen levels and control heavy bleeding symptoms. Some herbs provide an additional source of essential nutrients such as calcium, magnesium, and potassium that help relieve menstrual pain and cramps. Other herbs have mild relaxant, diuretic, and anti-inflammatory properties that help relieve painful symptoms with a minimum of side effects.

As mentioned in the vitamin section, bioflavonoids can help control fibroids and endometriosis. While purified bioflavonoids are available in capsule form, they are also a significant component of a wide variety of fruits and flowers. Bioflavonoids are responsible for the striking colors of many plants. Good sources of bioflavonoids include citrus fruits, hawthorn berries, bilberries, cherries, and grape skins. Bioflavonoids have also been found in red clover and in some clover strains in Australia. Many of these plants are available as herbal tinctures (liquid) or in capsules.

Two herbs that women traditionally used to stop excessive menstrual flow and postpartum hemorrhage are **goldenseal** and **shepherd's purse.** Goldenseal contains a chemical called berberine that calms uterine muscular tension. It has also been used to calm and soothe the digestive tract. Shepherd's purse promotes blood clotting and has been used to help stop menstrual bleeding. If your bleeding is excessive or irregular, consult your physician. This condition should be evaluated carefully by your physician and, if necessary, medical therapy should be instituted. Excessive and irregular bleeding can be dangerous and should never be allowed to continue without medical help. For those women for whom the menstrual flow is normal but somewhat heavier than usual, the mild properties of herbs may help relieve symptoms.

Other herbs help to prevent anemia by providing good sources of nonheme iron. Excellent examples are **yellow dock** and **pau d'arco.** Yellow dock is also used to promote liver health—an important factor in decreasing heavy bleeding through regulation of excessive estrogen levels, since the liver breaks down estrogen and prepares it for excretion from the body. **Tumeric,** or curcumin, is also used to promote liver health in traditional medicine. Recent research suggests that it has antibacterial properties. Turmeric is a delicious herb often used for flavoring in traditional Indian dishes. **Silymarin,** or milk thistle, protects liver functions through its flavonoid content. These flavonoids are strong antioxidants and help protect the liver from damage.

Anti-inflammatory Herbs. Several anti-inflammatory herbs may help relieve symptoms of endometriosis and reduce inflammation of implants. Both **meadowsweet** and **white willow bark** reduce inflammation, pain, and fever. They help treat primary menstrual cramps and menstrual headaches as well as the pain symptoms due to endometriosis, because they suppress the action of F_2 alpha prostaglandins. Unfortunately, like aspirin, they can produce the unwanted side effects of gastric indigestion, nausea, and diarrhea, so use these herbs carefully.

Essential Fatty Acids

Sufficient essential fatty acids are an extremely important part of the nutritional program for any women with menstrual cramps caused by endometriosis or fibroid tumors. As mentioned earlier in the book, fatty acids are the raw materials from which the beneficial hormonelike chemicals called prostaglandins are made. The prostaglandins from essential fatty acids have muscle-relaxant and blood-vessel-relaxant properties that can significantly reduce muscle cramps and tension. They also have an anti-inflammatory effect on tissues that is very important in limiting this deleterious response within the endometrial implants, thereby limiting painful pelvic symptoms.

There are two essential fatty acids, linoleic acid (Omega 6 family) and linolenic acid (Omega 3 family). They are derived from specific food sources in our diets, primarily raw seeds, nuts, and certain fish such as salmon, mackerel, and trout. Unlike the unhealthy saturated fats, these fats cannot be made by the body and must be supplied daily in our diets, through either food or supplements.

Even when these fatty acids are supplied in the diet, some women lack the ability to convert them efficiently to the muscle-relaxant prostaglandins. This is particularly true with linoleic acid, which must be converted to a chemical called gamma linolenic acid (GLA) on its way to becoming the series-one prostaglandin called E_1. The conversion of linoleic acid to GLA, followed by the chemical steps leading to the creation of the beneficial prostaglandins, requires the presence of magnesium, vitamin B_6, zinc, vitamin C, and niacin. Women who are deficient in these nutrients can't make the chemical conversions effectively.

In addition, women who eat a high-cholesterol diet, eat processed oils like mayonnaise, use a great deal of alcohol, or are diabetic may have difficulty converting fatty acids to series-one prostaglandins. Other factors that impede prostaglandin production include emotional stress, allergies, and eczema. In women with these risk factors, less than one percent of linoleic acid may be converted to GLA. The rest of the fatty acids can be used as an energy source, but they will not be able to play a role in relieving menstrual pain, cramp symptoms, and inflammation due to endometriosis.

Clinical studies have shown that the use of essential fatty acids can reduce most PMS symptoms by as much as 70 percent. Evening primrose oil, borage oil, and black currant oil are the most common supplemental sources of essential fatty acids for the treatment of menstrual cramps and PMS. All three oils contain high levels of GLA, allowing women to circumvent the difficult conversion process of linoleic acid to GLA.

The best food sources of essential fatty acids are **raw flax seed oil** and **pumpkin seed oil,** which contain high levels of both linoleic acid and linolenic acid, in combination. Both the seeds and their pressed oils should be used absolutely fresh and unspoiled. Because these oils become rancid very easily when exposed to light and air (oxygen), they need to be packed in opaque containers and kept in the refrigerator.

Fresh flax seed oil—golden, rich, and delicious—is my special favorite. Good quality flax seed oil is available in health food stores. Flax seed oil is extremely high in linoleic and linolenic acid, which comprise approximately 80 percent of its total content. Pumpkin seed oil has a deep green color and spicy flavor; it is probably more difficult to find than flax seed oil. A good source of this oil is fresh raw pumpkin seeds. The raw seeds can be purchased from a health food store and should be kept refrigerated because they are highly perishable. Both flax seed oil and pumpkin seed oil can also be taken in capsule form.

Linolenic acid (Omega 3 family) by itself is also found in abundance in fish oils. The best sources are cold-water, high-fat fish such as salmon, tuna, rainbow trout, mackerel, and eel. Linoleic acid (Omega 6 family) by itself can be found in seeds and seed oils. Good sources include safflower oil, sunflower oil, corn oil, sesame seed oil, and wheat germ oil.

Many women prefer to use raw fresh sesame seeds, sun-flower seeds, and wheat germ to obtain the oils. The average healthy adult requires only four teaspoons per day of the essential oils, although women with menstrual cramps may need several tablespoons per day. If you use whole flax seed, remember that the seeds are 50 percent oil by content, so you need twice as much whole seed intake as oil for the same amount of fatty acids. For optimal results, be sure to use these oils along with vitamin E. The vitamin E also helps to prevent rancidity of the oils.

PHYSICAL EXERCISE AND YOGA

You should do moderate exercise on a regular basis, at least three times a week. Aerobic exercise can improve both circulation and oxygenation to tight, constricted muscles, thereby helping you relax. It is important, however, to do your exercise routine slowly and comfortably. Frenetic exercise that is too fast-paced can push your muscles to the point of exhaustion and tense them further. Women with fibroid- or endo-metriosis-related pain and cramps need to keep their muscles and joints flexible and supple.

The uncomfortable symptoms of fibroids and endometriosis respond well to the gentle stretches of yoga. Yoga exercises that emphasize pelvic movement and flexibility can help treat the menstrual cramps, pelvic congestion, and low back pain that commonly occur with these two problems. Yoga may even help control heavy menstrual flow. The slow, controlled stretching movements that you do in these exercises help relax tense muscles and improve their suppleness and flexibility. They also bring better blood circulation and oxygenation to the tense areas of your lower body, thereby improving the metabolism of the pelvic and back muscles.

Yoga has an additional benefit in that it quiets your moods. The deep breathing and slow movements that characterize these exercises reduce anxiety and irritability and produce a sense of peace—a welcome change for women who have fibroids or endometriosis and also have significant life stress. The stress reduction effects of yoga benefit all body systems, including the reproductive tract and the immune system.

STRESS REDUCTION

Many of the fibroid and endometriosis patients I see in my medical practice complain of major stress along with their physical symptoms. In women with fibroids and endometriosis, stress may negatively affect hormonal balance and muscle tone, upsetting the estrogen and progesterone balance and triggering excessive output of adrenal stress hormones. This can impair the body's ability to limit the scarring and inflammation caused by the endometrial implants. Growth in the size of fibroid tumors is also seen during times of stress.

Stress in fibroid and endometriosis patients can arise over such issues as job security and performance, money worries, relationship problems with family and friends, overwork, and a host of other common problems. In addition, women with fibroids and endometriosis have specific stress due to the diseases themselves, including concerns about their health and about the painful symptoms that are disrupting their lives and well-being. The infertility that can result from fibroids and endometriosis is a particularly upsetting problem for women who are trying to start a family. The pain during intercourse that is also common in women with endometriosis can disrupt a healthy sexual relationship, causing anguish and discord.

A variety of stress management techniques can help women suffering from fibroids and endometriosis. Some women find counseling or psychotherapy to be effective, while others depend heavily on the support of family and friends. Many women find it helpful to rethink their way of handling stressful situations and to implement lifestyle changes. Practicing stress-reduction techniques like meditation and deep-breathing exercises on a regular basis also helps them handle stress more effectively, as does a program of physical exercise. Whatever methods you decide to practice, I urge you to look at your stress level carefully and make every effort to handle emotionally-charged issues as calmly as possible.

For further information on stress management techniques, physical exercise and yoga see my larger book, *Fibroid Tumors & Endometriosis*, (Westchester Publishing Co., Los Altos, CA; 1993) or one of the following books:

Benson, H., and M. Klipper. *Relaxation Response*. New York: Avon, 1976.

Gawain, S. *Creative Visualization*. San Rafael, CA: New World Publishing, 1978.

Kripalu Center for Holistic Health. *The Self-Health Guide*. Lenox, MA: Kripalu Publications, 1980.

Loehr, J., and J. Migdow. *Take a Deep Breath*. New York: Villard Books, 1986.

Ornstein, R., and D. Sobel. *Healthy Pleasures*. Reading, MA: Addison-Wesley, 1989.